VIRGIN

VIRGIN

poems

ANALICIA SOTELO

MILKWEED EDITIONS

The characters and events in this book are fictitious. Any similarity to real persons, living or dead, is coincidental and not intended by the author.

Published 2018 by Milkweed Editions
Printed in the United States of America
Cover design by Mary Austin Speaker
Cover photograph by L. Haase after H.W. Berend, 1859, courtesy of the Wellcome Library, London
Author photo by Brooke Lightfoot
18 19 20 21 22 5 4 3 2
First Edition

Milkweed Editions, an independent nonprofit publisher, gratefully acknowledges sustaining support from the Jerome Foundation; the Lindquist & Vennum Foundation; the McKnight Foundation; the National Endowment for the Arts; the Target Foundation; and other generous contributions from foundations, corporations, and individuals. Also, this activity is made possible by the voters of Minnesota through a Minnesota State Arts Board Operating Support grant, thanks to a legislative appropriation from the arts and cultural heritage fund, and a grant from Wells Fargo. For a full listing of Milkweed Editions supporters, please visit milkweed.org.

Library of Congress Cataloging-in-Publication Data

Names: Sotelo, Analicia, author.
Title: Virgin : poems / Analicia Sotelo.
Description: Minneapolis, Minnesota : Milkweed Editions, [2018]
Identifiers: LCCN 2017030827 (print) | LCCN 2017040484 (ebook) | ISBN
    9781571319777 (ebook) | ISBN 9781571315007 (softcover : acid-free paper)
Classification: LCC PS3619.O862 (ebook) | LCC PS3619.O862 A6 2018 (print) |
    DDC 811/.6--dc23
LC record available at https://lccn.loc.gov/2017030827

Milkweed Editions is committed to ecological stewardship. We strive to align our book production practices with this principle, and to reduce the impact of our operations in the environment. We are a member of the Green Press Initiative, a nonprofit coalition of publishers, manufacturers, and authors working to protect the world's endangered forests and conserve natural resources. *Virgin* was printed on acid-free 100% postconsumer-waste paper by Thomson-Shore.

To mom and dad, with all my love

Contents

VIRGIN

Do You Speak Virgin?

This wedding is some hell:

a bouquet of cacti wilting in my hand
while my closest friends

sit on a bar bench,
stir the sickles in their drinks, smile up at me.

The moon points out my neckline
like a chaperone.

My veil is fried tongue & chicken wire,
hanging off to one side.

I am a Mexican American fascinator.

Let me cluck my way to an empty field

where my husband stays silent
& the stars are the arachnid eyes

of my mother-in-law: duplicitous,
ever-present in the dark.

I'm not afraid of sex.

I'm afraid of his skeleton
knocking against the headboard

in the middle of the night.

I'm afraid I am a blind goat
with a ribbon in my hair, with screws for eyes.

I'm afraid wherever I walk, it's purgatory.

I meet a great lake with rust-colored steam
rising, someone somewhere

has committed murder, hides
in the bushes with an antique mirror.

~

The virgins are here to prove a point.
The virgins are here to tell you to fuck off.

The virgins are certain there's a circle of hell ·
dedicated to that fear you'll never find anyone else.

You know what it looks like:

all the lovers—cloaked in blood & salt
& never satisfied,

a priest collar like a giant tooth
in the midnight sky.

I want to know what's coming in the afterlife

before I sign off on arguments
in the kitchen & the sight of him

fleeing to the car

once he sees how far & wide,
how dark & deep

this frigid female mind can go.

TASTE

Summer Barbecue with Two Men

Tonight, the moon looks like Billie Holiday, trembling
because there are problems other people have
& now I have them, too.

I'm wearing a cherry-colored cardigan over
a navy print dress, on purpose.
People think I'm sweet.

I try the ancho chile pork ribs, in case
the man I once wanted might still
rub off on me.

I wonder if I'll ever know about flavors, what
tastes right. In the overheated kitchen,
I chat briefly with a series of

thirty-something-year-old men—all slender, all
bearded, lustful to the point of sullen.
I hug & compliment

their pretty female partners as a way of saying,
I am beautiful in my harmlessness!
Outside, people.

A circle of party chairs. I don't care much
for a stranger's guacamole. The man
I once wanted is grilling

these beautiful peaches. He offers some—
I'm embarrassed. I try not
to touch his hand.

I try to touch his hand. On the porch,
another man I know is kissing
the shoulder of a woman

whose fiancé is here somewhere. *Guess what,*
he says. *You're the only one who cares.*
I wouldn't have guessed:

judgment is a golden habañero margarita
with wings, wet & cold
on his chest. So

many people are tender from the right angle.
I'm hungry & confused. I love
a good barbecue. Save me.

A Little Charm

She floats like a lost brain cell.
Her body is a sleek brown lamp from 1929.
She arches and slurs.
Gentlemen in winter coats would like to cover her.
Gentlemen in thick winter coats hand her new cigars.
She nods like a child under the influence of milk.
She appeals with eyes as wide as money.
Even in alleys, her legs look like unfiltered honey.
Her moods are expensive. She's all lit up.
Gentlemen order her whiskey and whiskey
and horses dip her gloves
into the whiskey with their mouths.
They love her. They want to sweep her up
with their tongues until she learns to stand straight.
She never learns. I did not suspect I would like her.
I did not expect to give her
this loving little push out the door.

You Really Killed That '80s Love Song

Now someone else is kissing him
on a wrought iron balcony
above the karaoke bar,
and it's not animal
exactly, not pretty either,
the drunken howling behind you
as you act like you're not watching,
like you're talking on the phone
on a wet Texas night
instead of doing
what you should have done before.
Now it's raining harder.
Now you're driving home at 2 a.m.
on a road that's slick as sex
and you can still hear your friend David
saying there's no way you could be in love
if you've never been loved in the first place.
Now you're curled in bed.
Now the sun drifts to your knees.
You've discovered
humiliation is physically painful:
the crown-like stigmata of a peach
that's been twisted, pulled open,
left there. The juices must run somewhere.
You can't help but imagine the knife in his body,
her body. The pink, cloudy aubade
you were waiting for.

Expiration Date

All my acquaintances are coupled up
like hamsters with advanced degrees.

I like the children they haven't had and
the fine bourbon jam they're saving.

I'm a radish tonight, for everyone
has been flowering with careful hellos

and it's made me red and pungent,
made me sick of potluck drinking

under the stars with the weeds brushing
their blond hair against my ankles, sick

of the clear buttons of sweat on their skin
and their salty arguments about who's best

at breathing, who's better at playing nurse.
I am done with you, couples. We are

breaking up. I will see you on the floodwaters
in your restored pine boat, looking hard

for your Foucault, your baseball caps,
your grandmother's velvet couch,

but I will not stop for you because you always say, "Oh, us? We're *fine*. Everything's fine."

Apologia over Marinated Lamb

You say you're a hedonist.
You say God doesn't exist.
You say you like things when they're new
and that you're sorry. I'd rather
know nothing. Not about you,
not about me, not about nihilism or Dionysus.
All I know is that two people can disagree
about everything and still end up at lunch.
It's my birthday. Thank you for the meal.
I'm looking at the sea on the wall, and
even though it's a copy of a copy of the Aegean,
I wish you would grab me and take me to Greece.
I see you hanging a freshly killed lamb
from our open window, letting the blood
drip down the wall onto the cobblestone.
We are eating dolmas and roasted eggplant
in a small room where you tell me all your secrets.
You want to apologize for leading me on,
but I want a different apology. An apologia
for how I think of you: nonstop Godhead.
And I'm not sorry you're here and in front of me
and breathing and eating. If you're Bacchus,
where's my wine? Where were you
when I was naked, offering
a thousand dinners in my tiny kitchen?
How's my birthday lamb? Oh, brutal. Delicious.

Purgatory Tastes Like Eggs

A man walks into my kitchen in athletic shorts.

That's the joke—a man, in my kitchen.

"Can't sleep," I say when he gives me that look.

In a slip dress, I pierce two fried eggs with a fork.

2 a.m.: the sirens call, his pocket vibrates.

"Answer if you want," I say.

This is my humid kingdom, blades of bobby pins in my hair.

What do I care if I'm here with a stranger?

Like my father in the mirror in the middle of the night?

I slap another egg on the plate. He slips out for a smoke.

Hello father. Goodbye father.

When I'm with a man, I drag the yolk right out of him.

REVELATION

South Texas Persephone

Someday the ground will open up
and swallow me.

Someday I'll be swept

through the sand, and the grass
will become my crown

of burnt paper.

And he will be there: tall,
steel-toed, eyes like ice in whiskey,

handing me my first drink.

In the bar, we'll dance to a song I hate,
but I'll cling to him anyway.

This is the darkness of marriage,

the burial of my preferences
before they can even be born.

This is my set of sins reaching out

from a frozen lake, where
the smoke of his breath is interrupting.

Look now: my heart

is a fist of barbed wire. His heart
is a lake where young geese

go missing, show up bloody

after midnight. I don't say
a single thing.

My dress is deep green, knotted,

feathered at the seams.
O, isn't this

what my mother never wanted?

Now I have three heads: one
for speech, one for sex,

and one for second-guessing.

Revelation at the All-Girls School

Jackson: O Archangel, O '96 Triumph, O unfiltered
flame in hand. What was that joke you told the class
about the burning bush? The joke was *bush* & not
much more. The bad girls' legs were smooth as coconut
candles. I dreamt of melted wax. I prayed for the nicotine
shadow of your Pentecost. You paced the stage in your
Levi's, harness on, quoting Christopher Marlowe in
your Mississippi drawl. I was a clever rosary. You were
a layman's interpretation of the Law. What happened
with those girls? You said they didn't have fathers. Said
they needed you *like God*. Like I did, only I was strong.
That was the year I cared my father never called, the year
I fell in love & denied it. Who could I believe? So I tried
to recite your passionate shepherd's plea, but my sheep
became goats & my goats caught fire & they began
to bleat louder, right through the house: no applause.
Backstage all summer: *Kind of Blue*. Like worried notes,
they badly burned out for you. O Jackson, thou art sick.
O Jackson, thou art gone. Jackson: your wife's hair,
barley & rye, waving in the Coltrane—it doesn't make
sense, but it does. She had a small, pretty mouth, an edge
of sarcasm & a kind face like a clock in the country.

Private Property

In this minor emergency of the self,
we drink to become confused,
to swim in the dark like idiot fish.

This is a lake at night in a forest.

This is where we look up at the stains
in the sky and someone says, *It's purpling out here*,
and someone else says, *Someone write that down*.

We're all performing our bruises.

Chloe smiles like a specialty knife,
Bea tells stories like a bubbly divorcée,
Clara smokes like a sage in her coiffed towel,
expertly naked, third eye shining.

I hang back on the shore with Kyle.
We talk about his man in New York
while our skinny-dipping sirens
sing show tunes in the violet dark.

Later, we're all in a clinic at 3 a.m.
handling Kyle's broken ankle.
It's so embarrassing, he keeps saying.

And it is: earlier, doing the sprinkler
in a dorm room to *Please Don't Stop the Music*,
he kept yelling, *Stop the music! Stop the music!*
until we understood: he wasn't actually joking.

And sometimes the poems were like that.
When we wrote *knife*, *bubbly*, *naked*,
we were really getting down,
dancing hard on the injury.

Philosopher King

He said, "Once, when I thought of the
moon, I thought of luminous shelter.
Then I flew there, and I wasn't the only
man. Women in yellow tulle were riding
bicycles in the shadow of the sun while
men rode in on tiny black horses. I hate
how everyone is either a tiny black horse
or a big fat gnat, sans fucking purpose. I've
been reading *Fear and Trembling* all night,
and I thought of you reading in your room
with your parents asleep. You're innocent,
so maybe you won't believe me, but I
did this thing I never should have done,
which was throw a knife at my father,
and I thought you should know. I need
to clarify. There's more to this world than
movies and orchards. You know what I'm
saying. Let me sing you our song—I like
New York in June, how about you?"

I'm Trying to Write a Poem about a Virgin and It's Awful

She was very unhappy and vaguely religious so I put her at the edge of the lake where the ducks were waddling along like Victorian children, living out their lives in blithe, downy softness. She hated her idleness. I loved her resilience. Her ability to turn her gaze on small versions of herself seemed important. The lake wasn't really a lake. It was a state of mind where words like *ochre*, *darken*, and *false* were supposed to describe her at her best and worst, but they were only shadows and everyone knows the best shadows always look like the worst kinds of men. She wanted them badly, so I took her for a swim. In the lake that was not a lake, her twenty-five-year-old body felt the joy of being *bare* and *naïve* among the seaweed and tiny neon fish, but I didn't believe her. And I couldn't think of anything to say in her defense. Some people said I should take her out of the poem. Other people said no, take her out of the lake and put her in a bedroom where one man is saying, *I can't help you*, and another is saying, *You waited too long*. The men sounded like cynical seabirds. When they said *Virgin*, they meant *Version we've left behind*. I didn't trust them. So I took her to the rush of the sea. She waded in and waved at me. I turned away. It wasn't her fault. She wasn't the shell I was after.

HUMILIATION

Trauma with Damp Stairwell

There's no winter here in Texas
but the light changes, grows sharper,

keener, and when I was a girl,
it was breath to me,

walking up the hillside to school,
the wind touching my throat.

In the dreams I've had of him,
it is raining. I climb to the second floor

only to find him already gone.
The cool dark afternoon takes over.

He was the rain: he would come and go,
he was there for everyone.

Trauma with Haberdashery

Even now at the seawall:

I see the foam;
I see the bird's bones and feathers,
the mite-infested corset;
and what do I do?

I put on airs, stare too long
while the insects fatten up for the occasion.

I hold my breath.
I pose as if willing
to be ripped apart from the amygdala.

You make me feel I'm falling
into a ravine with children
dressed in felt flames.

Look at their chalkboard cheeks.
They're marked forever.

I am not saying I was marked,
I am saying I could have been and that is
stage-worthy trauma.

I touch my ribbons.
I think of you saying, *You're charming*,

with your anachronistic appetite

like a button that becomes a bird's eye on the sand

in this the twenty-first century
where men still love girls, but rarely admit it,
and history binds you to your signature.

Trauma with White Agnostic Male

> *And Holofernes took great delight in her*
> *and drank more wine than he had drunk at any time*
> *in one day since he was born.*
> —JUDITH 12:20

It's not too late now for me

to drive back to town,
to surprise you.

Meet me there: *the King William District, Fiesta.*

I'll wear strawberry ribbons
in my unkempt hair.

You'll mock a trio of mariachis,
a cer-vay-sa in your spidery hand.

That's how you'll say it: *Sir Vésa*
for love of my tender Latina outrage.

You loved it when I was sixteen

and you would love it now, my lips
a big red flower trembling

in the style of David Bowie

while you whisper *Christ cookies*,
Christ cookies in my indelicate ear.

This is blood
for blood, a prodigal heartbreak

I must return:

Artemisia is in one corner with her nursemaid;
my mother is in the other with a crushed velvet sack.

In a long black skirt, I'll mention
the jamaicas of my childhood,

my signature side ponytail, and how I,
brave on carbonated sugar and grilled meat,

always made it my mission to find my favorite teacher
amongst the booths, but which one?
And who am I?

The golden one.

Dear San Antonio native,
this is your little calf, talking.

Now I can stand here with your head
in my hands, or I can cut you off completely.

Either way: God forbid you live forever.

Trauma with a Second Chance at Humiliation

You remind me of a man I knew at sixteen.

Every afternoon,
I climbed the stairs to see him,

my copy of *The Sound and the Fury* clutched to my chest,
my hands fluttering with nerves.

When he said, *She was his whole world*,
about Caddy's kindness to Benji,

I thought, *How beautiful*,
the clocks stilling and the field widening—
his oblong figure behind the tree, hardly breathing.

I drew eyes in my notebooks that year,
wet lashes, dense pupils.

Also his figure—slender, awkward, geometric.

~

He
liked teasing me
and also a few others. But only I
read his copy of *The Dialogues*.

As I read, I felt him look.
At night, I traced his scribbled notes with my finger.

~

Eight years later,
I find a man who resembles him.

It's your encyclopedic mind.
It's the strangeness of your features.

It's the way you hold the burnt sugar to my mouth
to taste, then pull it away, eager for

my caramelized reaction.

~

Isn't it delicious?

There's always going to be someone
willing to give a spoonful

of their attention. The trick
is to recognize the conversation

will run out, right into
I'm sure we'll run into each other sometime.

~

That was in the bookstore,
the last time I saw him.

Now you are a page I read
while holding my breath. I'll turn you

into something else, a footnote
of a person. Like I was

sitting next to you
on our friend's couch,

your hand on my thigh for several seconds.
You said it—*Do you want me to cook for you?*

—as if you could promise that and more.

~

To admit I love you would be to admit

I love ideas more than men,
myself even less than ideas.

The thin line of your mouth,
I could have held it down, erased the

I didn't mean to make you think so.

~

What you don't say is an iris
locked in a container.

What I don't say is an iris
burning wildly over a pool of water.

I want you to take yours out.
Show it to me, please.

See how an object can change
when a new person wants it.

~

To divulge is dangerous, but it's also chimerical.

One side of me says, *Destroy.*
The other, *Be gentle.*

Now this pool of water is a platonic eye

that avoids attachment
by rippling away.

These ashen petals: the expectation
that you'll understand intuitively

what has taken me years to describe.

~

I'm open to ridicule.
I can let this go.

But just so you know,
after school, it was like this:

I sat on the desk,
we talked and talked.

You could say it was nothing,
the windows fogged with winter,

the trees outside
like the shadows of a bad idea

going brittle.

It does matter.
I don't have to tell you why.

PASTORAL

My Father & Dalí Do Not Agree

1981. June or August—the dry musk
of Laredo after a rain. In his parents' backyard,
my father slices a leaf of maguey, sketches it
with a Dutch attention to detail
no one in town has seen.
Enter Dalí. At first, he does not see
my father because Dalí is Dalí,
waltzing in from 1963 with his ocelot
to whom he speaks only French. Then
he does see: a sliver of a man
on a cement step, a gelatin print at dusk.
So he says, "Young man! Tonight, the moon! And above
the moon is an exquisite nude who is my mother
and my lover and my queen!"
"Leave," says my father. "I am working."
This is when Dalí turns into a fire ant
crawling from a brick hole to pinch my father awake.
Now it's 1992. The evening is harmless.
The smell of lard and corn is in the air.
I am five years old in the front yard
with the bougainvillea. My father
never remembers me, but I can see him
in the sky, in the negative space
between the brightly colored tissue.
Have I ever told you I am my mother's daughter?

I am not afraid to go back in time,
to have the moon reflected in my big brown eyes
as the terracotta roof arcs its terracotta arches.

My Father & de Chirico Asleep on Chairs
of Burnt Umber

I found them in the morning, fat as mules, walls
larger and more fantastic, one green ladder
leading into black, a window. All I knew about
my father then was that he drove a grey truck
or a white truck and was an artist. And he lived in Austin.
That night Giorgio had come all the way from 1913
to say that architecture is the absence of love,
but that's where we all want to live.
I watched linseed oil thicken into flat, misshapen tears
on my father's desk. A bare light bulb on a slight body: no
shade, nearly humanoid. Even the shadows had color,
a burnt umber. That night, I heard my father say
he'd made a type of bronze that could leave melancholy
on anyone it touched. Actually, the walls were ochre
as the afterlife, and by morning he wasn't there.

Picnic Pastoral (with Dark-Skinned Father)

In the dream, his new triplets
are floral and abundant.

In his arms, their blonde curls—
sun-flecked hay in the style of Pissarro,

which would mean
that he is their laborer, carrying them

through the fields, his skin
a furrow in the flax

where they grow: their bulbous white heads
sprouting soft and tender.

I see him as an inflorescence,
the darkly seeded hub of several petals,

and I am the one that fell off,

that would not wither. It's not
harvest here. That's why he's on time.

That's why he unloads the triplets
like sacks of threshed wheat

right on my blanket as I flail for something
to say, but he leans against a tree

like he has a headache, like his work
is never done, like it aches to say it:

I've been looking all over for you.

My Father Lost in a Game of Chess

I am facing a geometric board. I am cut and uncooked clay. The pawns announce me. I slope after them. The King is silent. Gott is silent. My father speaks in the voice of Nietzsche from behind a parapet. Nietzsche: so sensitive to light and sound that he lives in my father's studio, hands in shea butter gloves, head under a black umbrella. We are not in my father's studio. We are in a yellow living room. The knight, with his horse teeth, sings me his troubadour song. I question his motives. I insist control. The Queen says, *Go*, but I need to hear it from the King. Open his mouth. See what's left: a handful of doves bathed in their own oil and roasted. I eat the doves before he can mount me. I stick the tiny bones in his ears. Where is my father? Give him back to me. He grunts, *O Gott, O Gott, O Gott*. Reverence is a lost art. I angle him like the bishop.

Father Fragments (or, Yellow Ochre)

I was with my father for a whole weekend, the first

and last time. The sun scattered over the striated cement

as my mother nervously   clasped my hand. We

left her: the roads

became a room with only one lamp—

He smelled of clay and soft eraser,

and I did not know him,   but I loved him

like I loved my heartbeat,

that original invisible companion.

~

Everything between the years of three and five
was filled with one color: yolk

ran through the hallways like a trial of light.

~

All the other colors: muted:

      like me, around my relatives.

Their distorted faces were loud coins
I couldn't understand   But
my father—

I used to imagine him swimming through copper
just to get to me.

And we would have a celebration there
                    —our two minds reunited in the yard

Actually I was a child; I imagined him cinematically lifting me.

      ~

I held my mother's vessel:

Be careful
Be careful
Don't talk to anyone
Don't let him out of sight

I mean a five-year-old can only be one

of two things: careful or

too careful, right?

~

Wishing I could remember where we were going
on that trip that tunnel of shadows
chess games   relatives
then road
then nothing then no one
a hallway of amniotic light
a large woman saying everything
is fine but I remember the room the hardwoods
the mattress the one yellow lamp and my father there
just before I slept I wish I could remember where
we were going my father and I were going
somewhere

~

At the museum,
we pass the garden first,
walk under steel rectangular limbs,
push off the deadweight of the mansion doors.

The place, like me, had its visitation days.

My father loved it | My mother loved it

the iconography on the second floor | had high arches
and in those arches | a family | and sequestered there too
a chastening swallow | with eyes like ticking globes
so | the child looked from one to the next carefully
at the wooden eye sockets | the century'd dust | asked
why is this like this | why keep things this way | we have
to know what happened | was their answer each time

~

He did come back that day, but the memory was already made.

Wake up,
said my mother,
and the bed lifted into

my later years.

Wake up, says some man,
and I fall hard

onto the mattress where I wake

in a panic again

but he's right outside.
Not right for me, but right outside.

~

The room where my father left me was the idea of room—

four walls, one mattress, and he,

the idea of father,
the absence of room.

For years I felt the ghost of someone not dead in every gallery.

Father—with his cool, bronze heart.

~

Which one is better? he says.

I choose the nineteenth-century bust
with the kind eyes, hair curling
like a necklace at the nape,

because I think she is delicate like me,
but I do not wish to say it.

That one is conventional, he says.

He explains *conventional,*
how it takes the lines
of our original beauty and erases it.

He points out the sharp, irregular lines of the other,
says *patina* with care, like it's a woman's name.

This one is art. This is what art looks like.

~

My stepfather and I listening to music on country roads
after middle school football games:

How did midnight feel like safety?

So much so that I could call him dad
and never stop wanting to call him dad?

He previewed each song with a translation I could understand:

One man after another mistakes music for life.
Maybe he sacrificed something to be my father, but thank God.

~

I remember: the room was too hot.
The woman in the hallway was heavyset, German. Kind?
The hallway was one long exposure.

How can I tell you what it was like (four years old)
to sleep with my father by my side?
Like the only thing I'd ever wanted.

You may wish to make some connection
between father and lover here, as if your joke
could really be my life's solution, or as if

I haven't already done that, in a cuter way.
Many men have questioned my ability to sleep well
with anyone. But I was frightened of the room,

not of my father. Because the room was art itself
and I knew my father would always come back to it,
just as I would always come back to this room, this window.

MYTH

Ariadne Discusses Theseus in Relation to the Minotaur

When a man tells you he's a monster,
believe him.

      When a man says
you will get hurt,

leave. Get into
a boat,   out

onto a sea that everyone owns.
                      Who cares.

Look,

he touched the curls of his hair
before touching mine.

I didn't question him   until all the thread was gone.

Ariadne's Guide to Getting a Man

First, you must feel that no one could love you ever.
Let the feeling become a veil of black paper.
Let the paper become papier-mâché.
Make the mâché into marionette monsters.
Make the monsters fall in love and scold them
      when they disappear down the hallway.
When your friends look for husbands
      with muscles, horns, and hooves,
        make a face like you ate something tart,
like their taste in men is beastly.
Grow up some, but not with your body.
The book you are reading is about a girl who rejects a god.
The book you are reading is about a girl no one believes.
Consider loving a clever man with a multisyllabic name,
      a name you could trust,
      like Sophocles, Socrates, Thucydides—
      all soft at the edges and likely
to appreciate your stretches of languorous study.
You are at a drama festival in a sundress, eating honey cake.
Where are they?
Grow up even more, to the point where nothing fits.
Call a young doctor to help diagnose the problem.
He'll give you a bottle called:
   Dr. Naxos's Remedy for Acute Neuralgia.
Take it with egg white and saffron after a night dream.
Do you trust him? No, but everyone has left you
      to take in the country air.

Three nights later, you see him again—
        his tall, crepuscular body separates itself from the lilies.
And you realize the body is not grotesque—that it is, in fact,
        like a bolt of fine batiste gathered in your hand,
            but first you must give up
            a willingness to be right about the world.
Your brother is howling.
Your brother is howling
because your mother chose love and look where it left her.

Death Wish

Finally Theseus said it.

It was after he punched the door
and crowned his fist with bruises, after

he showered for the first time in days,
gingerly like a raccoon,

his dollar shaver suddenly jumping ship,
delicate from his "shaving cream's sea-foam touch,

Kanye's "Heartless" playing on loop,

door open, steam on every surface;
after his mother called via FaceTime

and his therapist via Skype, and he was hopeful,
and I was hopeful, and we were late to every party

because he was bleeding, bleeding from
his head to his hands,

like Christ without clear cause.

O that his arms could shine
like shields at some local Subway,

slamming tubs of antibiotic meat
before the middle class who hope to be happy. Surely

he would miss the cashmere call of the Banana Republic,

and the pills hopping like cuff links in his hand,
and the women who are desirable

because they're both sweet
and mean. Like him when he said,

I want to die,

from a position of great advantage.

Theseus at the Naxos Apartment Complex, 6 a.m.

This is no aubade. This is
a ship sailing into you
then breaking off
faster than you think.
This is Experience speaking:
what you need is a man
who will carve you
like a thick slab of marble
in his stable, idiot hands.
I like your little black slip though,
and the way you wash your face,
like something good is about to happen. I'm only good
at killing what I know, then taking off. So take it off
if you want to. They can't say I didn't warn you.
I wasn't made for morals.
I was born to do things right.

Ariadne at the Naxos Apartment Complex, 10 a.m.

If I call this *a garden*,
it's a garden. It's a marbled affair—

the A/C units dripping green-black rivers,

the residue of last night's rain
sitting in a cheap cherub's eye

while an imbalanced neighbor in a sun hat
tends sweetly to her basil.

If I call this *the antithesis of alone*, it is—

the ticking of his father's wind-up watch,
the flash of beer cans
lined irregularly on the counter

as I step outside into the rays
as if I was born heliotropic.

This day is proof
that there is a sundial
for every single decision throughout history,

and a garden is a garden
once you name it,

once you call it
by its Christian name.

I don't expect you to fall for my logic. I don't fall
for anyone's. I am here with him
because I want evidence.

Except the light is blind this morning
like a child at a funeral

asking, *What are we all standing here for?*

Ariadne Plays the Physician

We must set this story straight.
We must say there is another angle

to this foreign particle

lodged in my ribs like a small ivory
tiger or a Chinese lamp, the oil

coating my bones. Theseus,
you know you didn't break me.

I was the one who came to you
with a magnifying glass,

needing my Oxford credits

for the University of *Someone Wants Me*:
my gold-sealed social stigma.

I made my own marks. & everyone
should know it—I have an A+

in the humours of you. I was
an Edison bulb in a child's bedchamber,

a Spanish fan flirting with fire,

smoking as pity turned to shock
at mediocre parties where conversations

are weak with the ordinary.
My outfit betrayed me—you wept

right through my clinical gloves like
a little boy with a bad heart & a mean streak.

I monitored your ailments, but my logic
was circular: *What is man? What is*

man? What is this man doing here
with me? No bright conclusion.

I was bad at doctoring the truth.
I was in it for myself. & the skull

I carried in my hand in case
anyone took record? Still on my fingers.

PARABLE

My Mother as the Voice of Kahlo

I am fourteen & feeling ugly

looking at a unibrow
like the one I'd like to get rid of

when my mother says

Yes   it's supposed to be a bird
See   she did it on purpose
See   she didn't care

what people thought of her
only   what they were made of
which animals   were inside & why

Here   she's a stag in mid-leap

with nine arrows in her body
              alive   bleeding

Her grief is constant & irreparable

like the crown of fresh flowers
she killed   each day

See   the instinct for painting is the instinct for power

Women don't
choose work over love
but it's not the same for men

See   all men are in love with themselves

Like Diego   & your father

& even an artist
will leave his wife behind

but he can't   if she runs harder
if she's both   hunter & sacrifice

The Minotaur Invents the Circumstances of His Birth

I am born: her birthing dress is a mast in my mouth,

a moth wrecked in specks of sarcophagus black,

a parasol in the twelve-armed wheel of a phaeton,

a crinoline smoking in a fragrant fire—

I crawled through her human body

to meet her spectators head on

& in the high forceps of the evening

I said hello to my mother & they all fell down

Not my mother, lovely liar, upright with her hair down

I have her fine Georgian teeth & miniature eyes,

inherit her love of disguise

and the men that I eat—their monocles taste sweet

O Mother, this is heaven: I am sent to this earth to save you

My Mother as the Face of God

For now, we are both alive.

Another Sunday afternoon: I'm looking out
your bedroom window, looking down

at the cars speeding like stars in daylight

as you imagine they'll asteroid
right through our wooden fence,

burn up the roses you carefully planted—
the ones that stand delicately

as if for a picture
where someone is missing from the family reunion,
but no one wants to talk about it.

This is eternity.
I make fun of your children's garden:

a wrought iron table with matching chairs,
a bronze rabbit, curious as taxidermy,
a tea set without tea.

*I think I just saw
one of your ghost children
running around out there*, I say.

I'm morbid and loving. You made me.

You pay bills on a quilted blanket
while I picture them—their eyes

flashing; their cheeks a dark, daguerreotype silver;
their mouths, accidental knife marks on a paper plate.

Mother, your likeness is not easy
or accidental. I am trying to understand it, trying

to become the opening
your light projects painfully through.

The Minotaur's Letter to Ariadne

Like a buttercup was your heart in my hand
in the field when we were children
Crown myrtle in your hair,
a gurgling song
Then you grew
delicate as an ox,
obstinate as a—It was you
who taught me metaphor,
said, *Mother is a door*
I said, *What does that mean?*
All those years I misheard the men
say, Your mother is a whore,
thinking it was
something that swung open
so almost anything could enter
Oh sister, do not go
Like a buttercup was your heart in my hand

Separation Anxiety

Every afternoon, it's the same
womb of inattention:

the umbilical cord snaps, the lights go out,
and the residue of a failed relationship

lives on all my dishes.

When I was young, my mother
made a house of thin, papery walls.

Like handmade veins,
lit by tea light.

My dolls walked through the living room

and into the kitchen
where my biological father

dislocated their arms, arranged them
on the countertop for the sake of his plastic art.

You never know what a person is like

beneath his skin, what he'll do
with what's available.

When I feel for men, I forget her,
set the death clock going.

I want her to live on

so long, so well—I'd kill them first,

hang them from their sleeves
on planter hooks out the window, shut it tight.

And when it rained, I'd watch their arms
reach out boyishly toward the clouds,

toward the nebulae of *You're So Naïve.*

If she dies, I'll leave her silhouette
to dry on wooden clips in the backyard;

I'll sit out there in her cotton dress for the company.

My Mother & the Parable of the Lemons

Men do nothing for me. I forget
they're even there.

But I can't forget the tree
that half-died every summer,

the lemons like sour eggs
left unhatched by a pile of bricks.

That was the lesson:

Apá with his women in Mexico,
Amá with her chickens here.

She snapped the head right off,
chewed on the neck bone

while he drank his caldo by the bowl.

That's what marriage is like, you know,
someone is always well prepared

for the sacrifice, and someone else
is the sacrifice.

When I met your father, it was like that.

He said I could draw a lamp
better than most people,

better than my father never said I could,
and when I did,

all the chickens clucked their way
back to life, all the lemons

levitated to their original leaves.

But when you were born, the rind
broke—I chose you

over him. It was easy.

If you do marry, marry well
or marry never.

And remember:

a mother will always love you,
but a man can draw you in.

REST CURE

Fast Track

The babies are beautifully abstract.

In the dream, I am given three.

I kiss their sweet, ruddy cheeks.

I make midnight runs for formula.

Of course I have no husband!

Back home, they're fine.

They're playing on my twin bed.

That's what happens when bad luck

hands you someone else's babies.

They think your bed is their playground,

a field that drops into space,

and they are the astronauts and you

are the gravity, pulling them

back from the edge

by their diapers just in time.

In their soft helmets, they laugh.

They say, *Again! Again!*

A blank, thick-cut

poster lands in my lap. *What's this?*

Meet the milky amnesia of parenthood.

My brain's gotten fuzzy.

I can't remember

and then I do remember:

babies—but it's too late. *What's this?*

Just drop it. I'm there

at the edge just in time

to see its neck snap, head

crushed against body. I cup it

with my hand. It's a featherless pigeon.

I lay it on a heap of mounting trash

in the back of some building.

I'm a mess, and it isn't even funny

how in dreams, there can be more

than two truths. Like how, just now,

there are three babies back in my arms.

What's this? This mourning is mine forever.

The Single Girl's Rest Cure

The fiancés were like physicians
                                cutting right down to the diamonds
They said love is like milk
                                spilling everywhere
They said love is like steak
                                it's best when rare
They said help yourself now
                                before your stock runs out

I said: *I'm twenty-five on purpose*
I said: *I'm hungry, but not that hungry*
I said: *There's the grave, there it is*

holding a bouquet of weeds, proposing a life together

They said relax

They said   relax
                  sleeping helps   & later,   gardens & newborns

I said: *I'm getting out of here*   I said: *You're all divorcing*

They said what about strawberries & cream
They said what about codependency   it isn't that bad
They said don't read into it   just be careful what you read

I said: *I am careful*   *that's what I'm here for*

My English Victorian Dating Troubles

I am bad with men

because I am deeply holy: they see

right through me, they know

I wish to please.

They say I have a petticoat of needs.

Let's ruffle up some pillow feathers.

Let's see what they look like

laid out on the beach like

striped seagulls

after scraps

of my native tongue.

Out here, where the sand is so white,

so Westernized, how could I not

sink into it

& burn with questions

like what am I doing here

I am in the wrong book

I am in the wrong era

I am not Dorothea

I am Analicia

Why does the twenty-first century feel like this?

Like men are talking into

their favorite phonograph

& the phonograph is me

receiving their baritone: *You're so exotic*

Watch out, men, says my violin

I am a Royal Bengal man-eating tiger

I will devour your pith helmets

as well as these enchiladas

piled high with American mozzarella any time of day

See, there is a white man

in every single one of us.

Yes, everyone is wearing casual yacht wear now

& mispronouncing their specialty condiments

O gentlemen

I am the angel/whore of kale chips

I like to purchase as I please

I am completely in character

So I will accept your pearls

though I may cut them off with my teeth

& watch them slip down to the sea

into the kind woman

you've invented

for your own troubled purposes.

The Ariadne Year

When I sleep,
I don't dream of Theseus,
I dream of my father's copper head
extended over a jury,
books piled high—
heavy as eyelids,
flaps clamped shut.
I dream the scent
of my mother's lipstick
has come back to haunt me—
like an oil pastel
marking
my dreary, dramatic heart.
There's my bedroom now: the child-me
unreleased from the staircase
of history's incredible spine.
Theseus? What a joke.
A pawn, a plaything,
a custom doll.
I touch his soft hair.
I tell him things, expecting
he won't talk back,
but he is talking,
he is always talking,
he is talking only of himself,

he is saying there's no way
I'm ready for this kind of christening.

WINTER

Melancholy is sleeping hard
with one arm over her head,
the other
tucked under her neck,
expecting someone will notice.
She is a monastery—
her great arches sound out
with every footstep.
We know you're not real,
chant the men,
sliding their gloves
into their pockets.
The flowers they never left
were the color of persimmons
or the medieval heart
of the Virgin Mary.
Now that the kind nun is gone
(she was teaching me
to sight-read, to smile
at strangers in the street),
I pretend to play the piano
like a virtuoso
in my stained nightshirt,

estimating the minor notes
will hold the most attention,
but it's the major notes
I play when no one is watching.
They sound better than they did before.

SUMMER

O men,
your useless pink smiles
float like the aura of a migraine
on this weekend afternoon.
Let us not get coffee.
Let us not sit so close to each other
that we can't tell which thoughts
are truly private. I am tired
of undressing to no comment,
years and years of youth
wasted to the particles in the air.
I take back
what I said—come here
with your unplaceable frustration,
let me add it to my calendar
of knife-like headaches,
let me kiss you if I want
for months at a time.

FALL

What happens
when you have a name
that's so distinct,
men turn to you
and repeat it,
try to make it sound
as clean as it sounds to them?
A name they can't forget
even if they wanted to,
even if their ship meals turn sour
and the ocean hits hard, leaving a bruise.
They could forget your hair, your face,
the smell of your skin, but not
your name that returns
even as they let it go.
Her bed is an island,
her dreams are a breakthrough,
each vessel finds the pia mater,
sends her to the beach
to collect their driftwood. Burn it.
This is how I find you.

Acknowledgments

Thank you to the editors of the following publications, in which these poems first appeared:

Antioch Review: "I'm Trying to Write a Poem about a Virgin and It's Awful"

Bennington Review: "The Minotaur Invents the Circumstances of His Birth"

Boston Review: "My Mother & the Parable of the Lemons," "My Father & Dalí Do Not Agree," "Picnic Pastoral (with Dark-Skinned Father)," "My Father Lost in a Game of Chess," and "Trauma with White Agnostic Male"

The Collagist: "Do You Speak Virgin?"

Copper Nickel: "Trauma with Haberdashery" and "My Mother as the Face of God"

Devil's Lake: "The Single Girl's Rest Cure"

FIELD: "Ariadne at the Naxos Apartment Complex, 10 a.m." and "Theseus at the Naxos Apartment Complex, 6 a.m."

Forklift, Ohio: "Fast Track" and "My English Victorian Dating Troubles"

Gigantic Sequins: "Trauma with Damp Stairwell"

Grist: "The Minotaur's Letter to Ariadne"

Horsethief: "Purgatory Tastes Like Eggs"

Indiana Review: "Ariadne Discusses Theseus in Relation to the Minotaur"

Iowa Review: "My Mother as the Voice of Kahlo"

Jet Fuel Review: "Trauma with a Second Chance at Humiliation"

Kenyon Review: "Ariadne Plays the Physician"
Meridian: "Revelation at the All-Girls School" and
    "Ariadne's Guide to Getting a Man"
Missouri Review: "South Texas Persephone"
New England Review: "The Ariadne Year"
The New Yorker: "Death Wish"
Quarterly West: "Expiration Date"
Subtropics: "A Little Charm"
Texas Review: "Separation Anxiety"
Waxwing: "Summer Barbecue with Two Men,"
    "You Really Killed That '80s Love Song," and
    "Apologia over Marinated Lamb"
West Branch: "My Father & de Chirico Asleep on Chairs of
    Burnt Umber"

Thank you Rigoberto González for selecting some of these
poems as *Nonstop Godhead* for the 2016 Poetry Society of
America Chapbook Fellowship.

Thank you Tracy K. Smith for selecting "I'm Trying to
Write a Poem about a Virgin and It's Awful" for *Best New
Poets 2015*.

Thank you Justin Chrestman, Christopher Lucas, and
Karyna McGlynn for reading me and these words so closely,
and to Adrienne Fisher, Janine Joseph, Elizabeth Lyons,
Nick McRae, Celeste Prince, Regina Román, and Sarah
Tamayo for your friendship and support. Thank you Justin
Brasher, Ruben Dupertuis, Katie Hays, Patricia Spears Jones,

Luis and Rebecca Murillo, Andrew Porter, Rita Urquijo-Ruiz, and G.C. Waldrep for the encouragement.

Thank you Tony Hoagland, Kevin Prufer, Roberto Tejada, Alex Parsons, and the University of Houston Creative Writing Program.

Thank you to the Community of Writers at Squaw Valley, the Image Text Ithaca Symposium, the Bucknell Seminar for Younger Poets, and the Poison Pen Reading Series for your incredible artistic communities.

Thank you to the insightful, energetic staff at Milkweed Editions for putting this book into the world with such great care.

Thank you Ross Gay for seeing the beauty in heartbreak.

Thank you to my parents, Linda and Steve, and my sister, Marissa, for always saying I could. Thank you to Grandma Gonzalez and Aunt Tere, for being there and letting me read as much as I wanted. Thank you, Ama and Apa. Que dios te proteja.

And finally, thank you, reader. Thank you, poems!

Brooke Lightfoot

ANALICIA SOTELO is the author of *Nonstop Godhead*, selected by Rigoberto González for a 2016 Poetry Society of America National Chapbook Fellowship. Her poems have appeared in the *New Yorker, Boston Review, Kenyon Review, New England Review, FIELD*, and elsewhere. "I'm Trying to Write a Poem about a Virgin and It's Awful" was selected for *Best New Poets 2015* by Tracy K. Smith. A graduate of the MFA program at the University of Houston, Sotelo is the recipient of the 2016 Disquiet International Literary Prize in Poetry and scholarships from the Community of Writers at Squaw Valley and the Image Text Ithaca Symposium. She lives in Houston.

The Jake Adam York Prize for a first or second collection of poems was established in 2016 to honor the name and legacy of Jake Adam York (1972–2012). York was the founder of *Copper Nickel*, a nationally distributed literary journal at the University of Colorado Denver. His work as a poet and scholar explored memory and social history, and particularly the Civil Rights Movement.

The judge for the inaugural 2016 Jake Adam York Prize was Ross Gay.

milkweed
editions

Founded as a nonprofit organization in 1980, Milkweed
Editions is an independent publisher. Our mission is to
identify, nurture and publish transformative literature,
and build an engaged community around it.

milkweed.org

Interior design by Mary Austin Speaker
Typeset in Adobe Caslon
by Mary Austin Speaker

Adobe Caslon Pro was created by Carol Twombly for
Adobe Systems in 1990. Her design was inspired by the
family of typefaces cut by the celebrated engraver
William Caslon I, whose family foundry served
England with clean, elegant type from the early
Enlightenment through the turn of the
twentieth century.